Playing

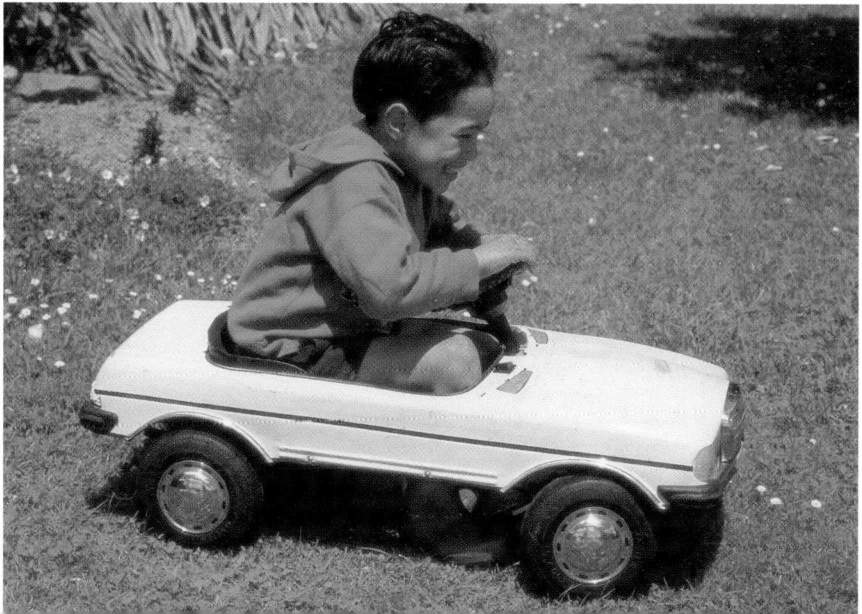

I am in the box.

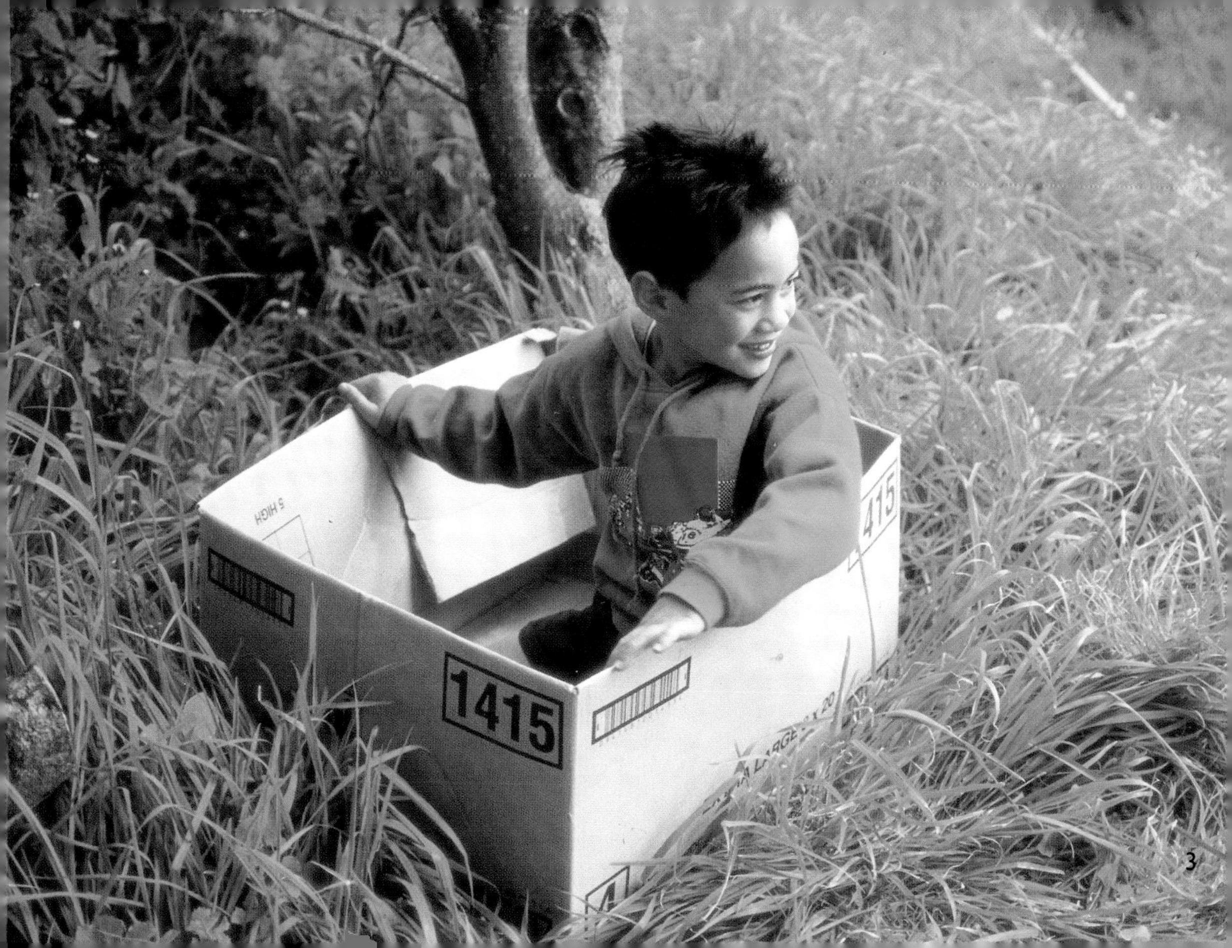
1415

I am in the car.

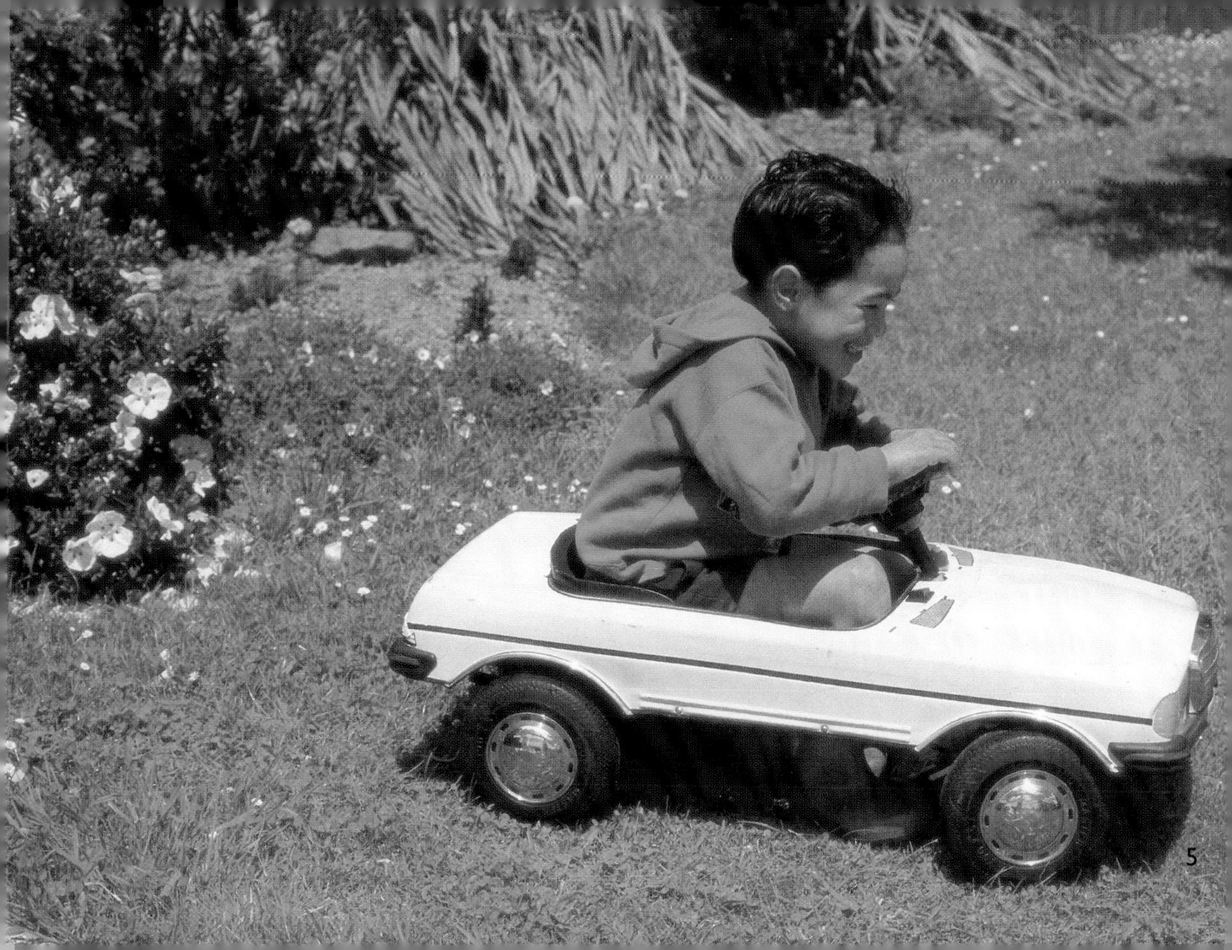

I am in the tent.

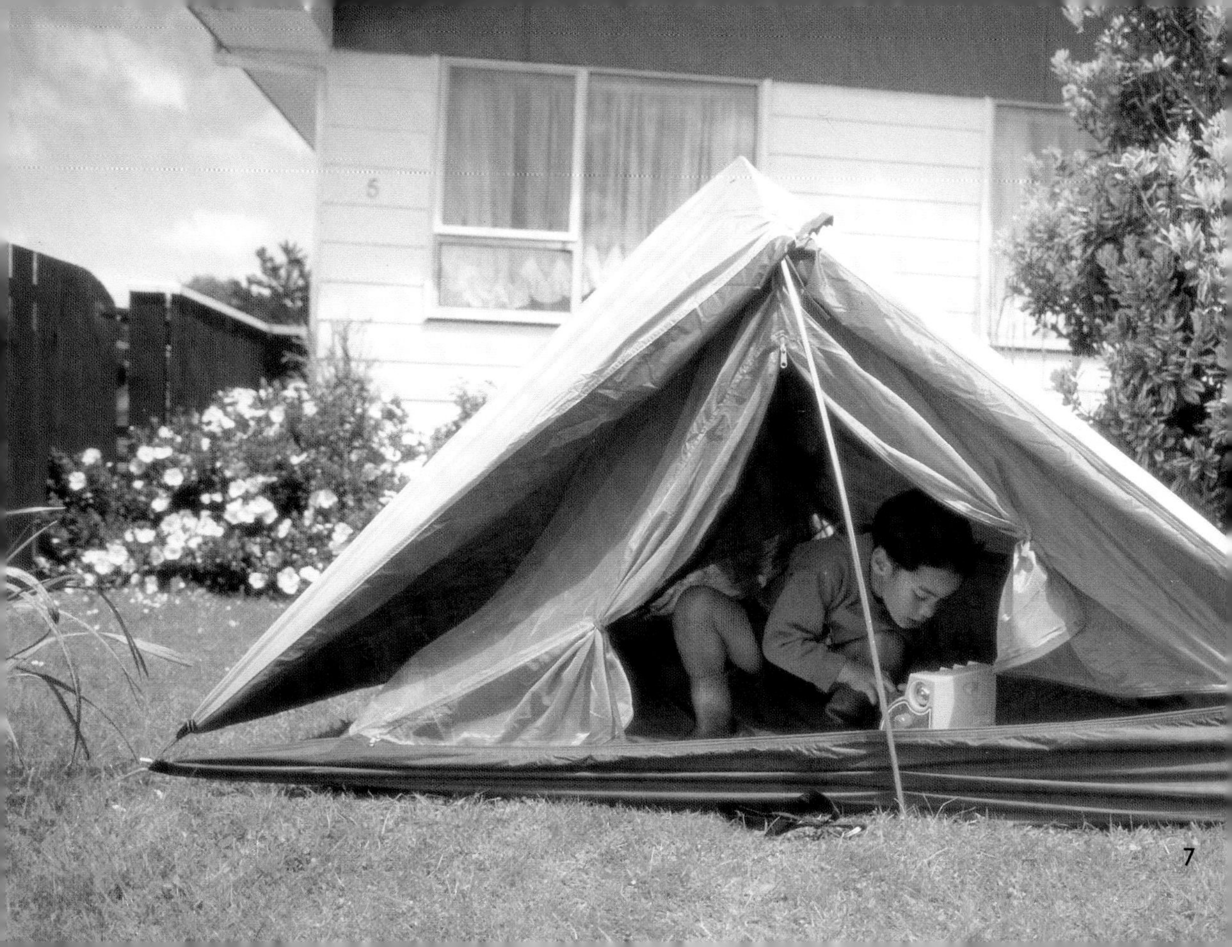

I am in the sandbox.

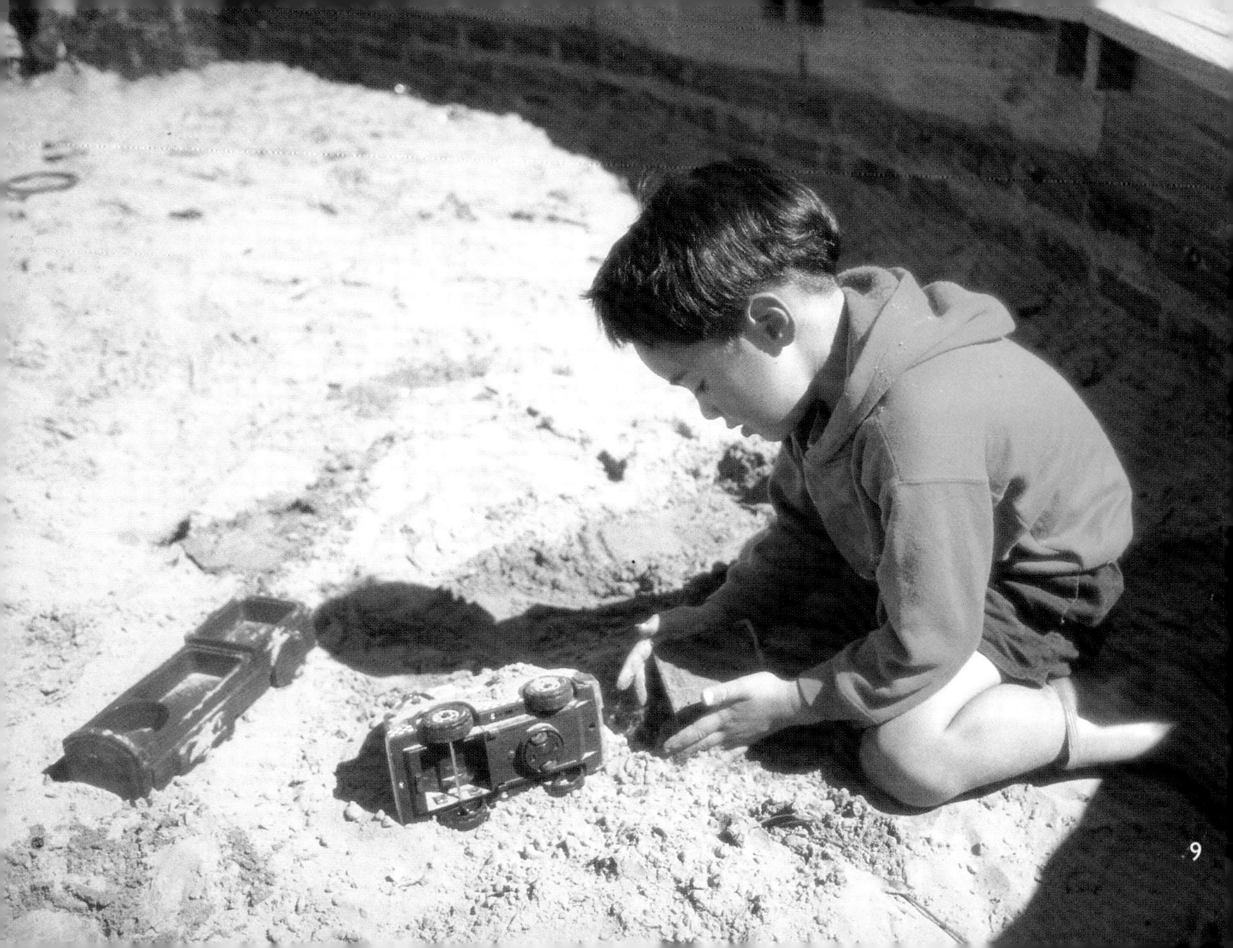

I am in the playhouse.

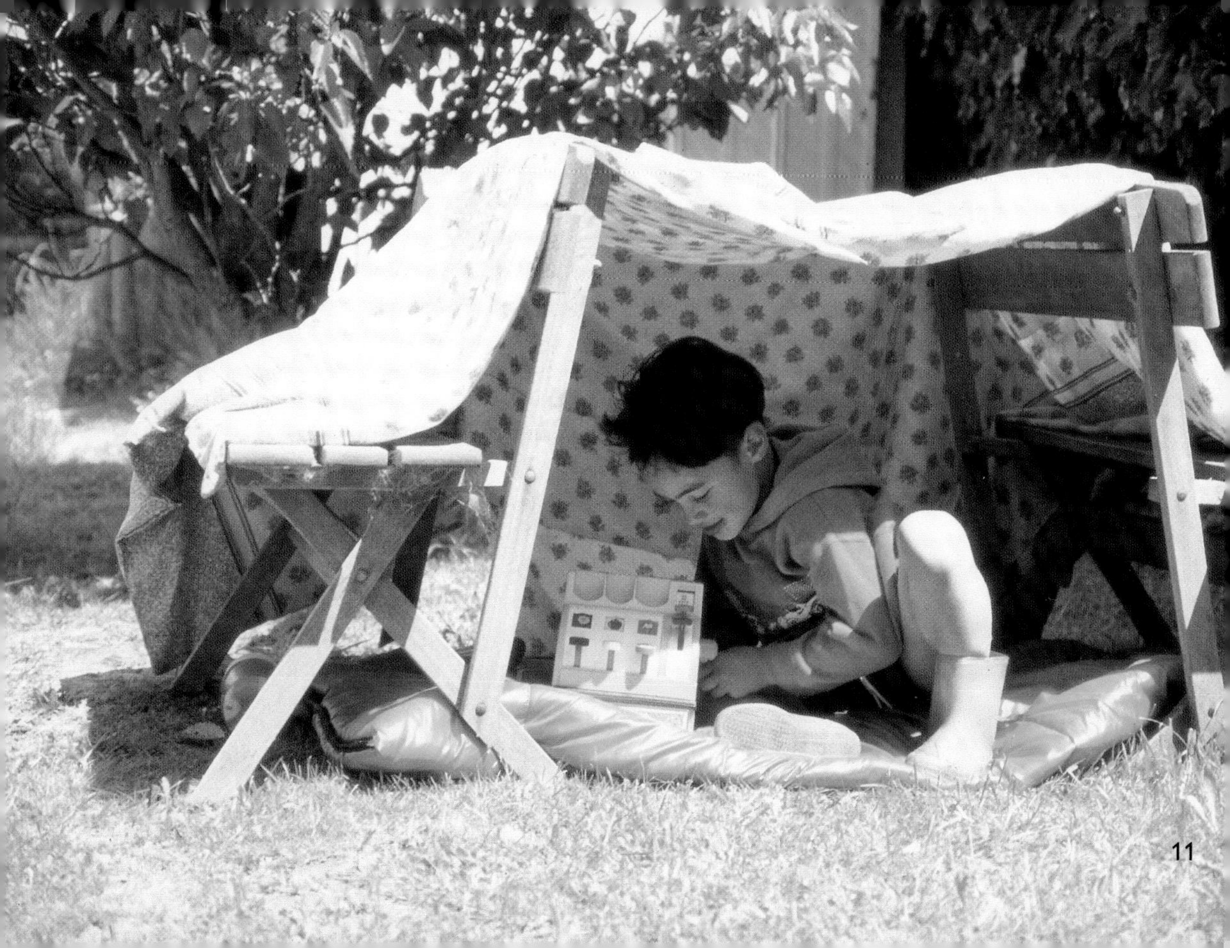

I am in the tree.

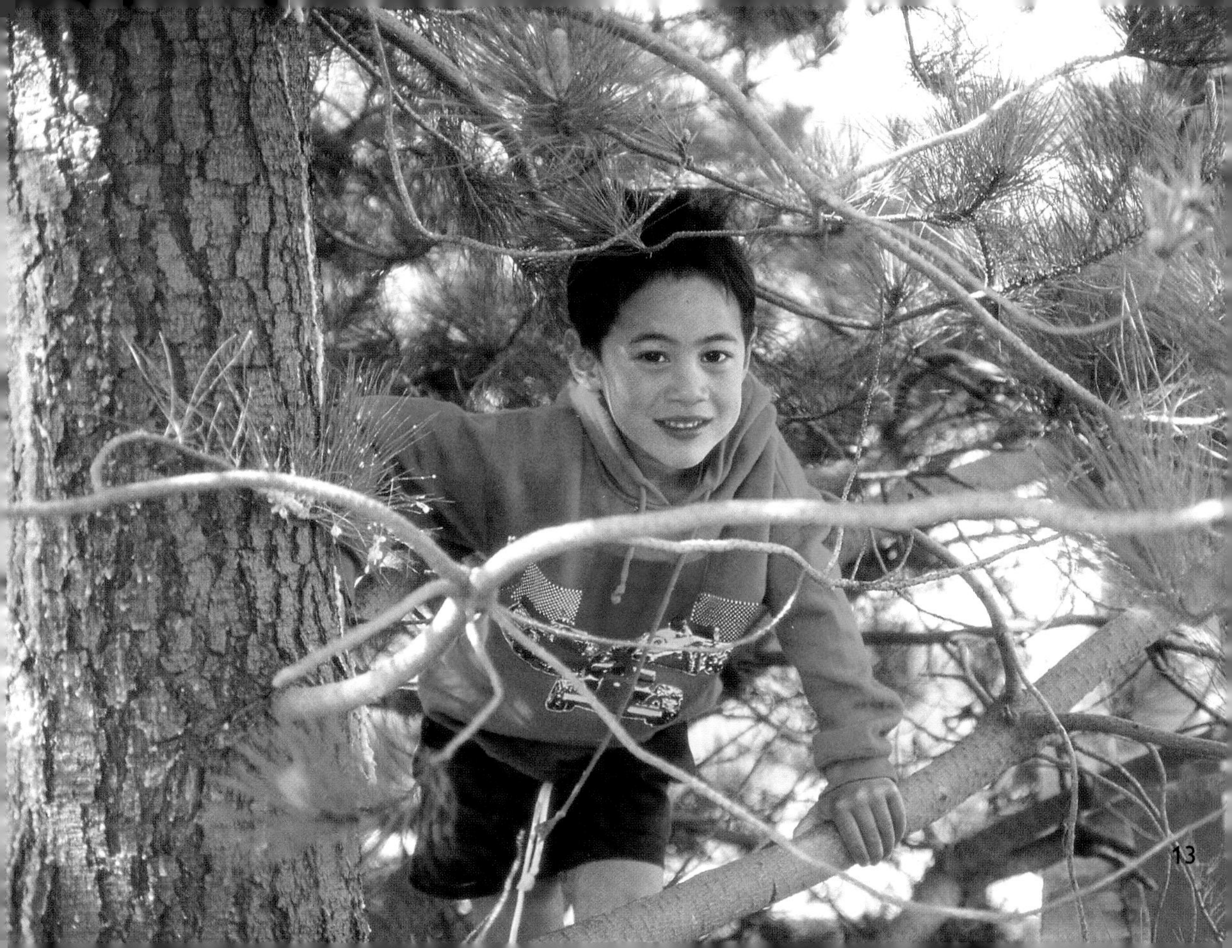

I am in the bathtub.

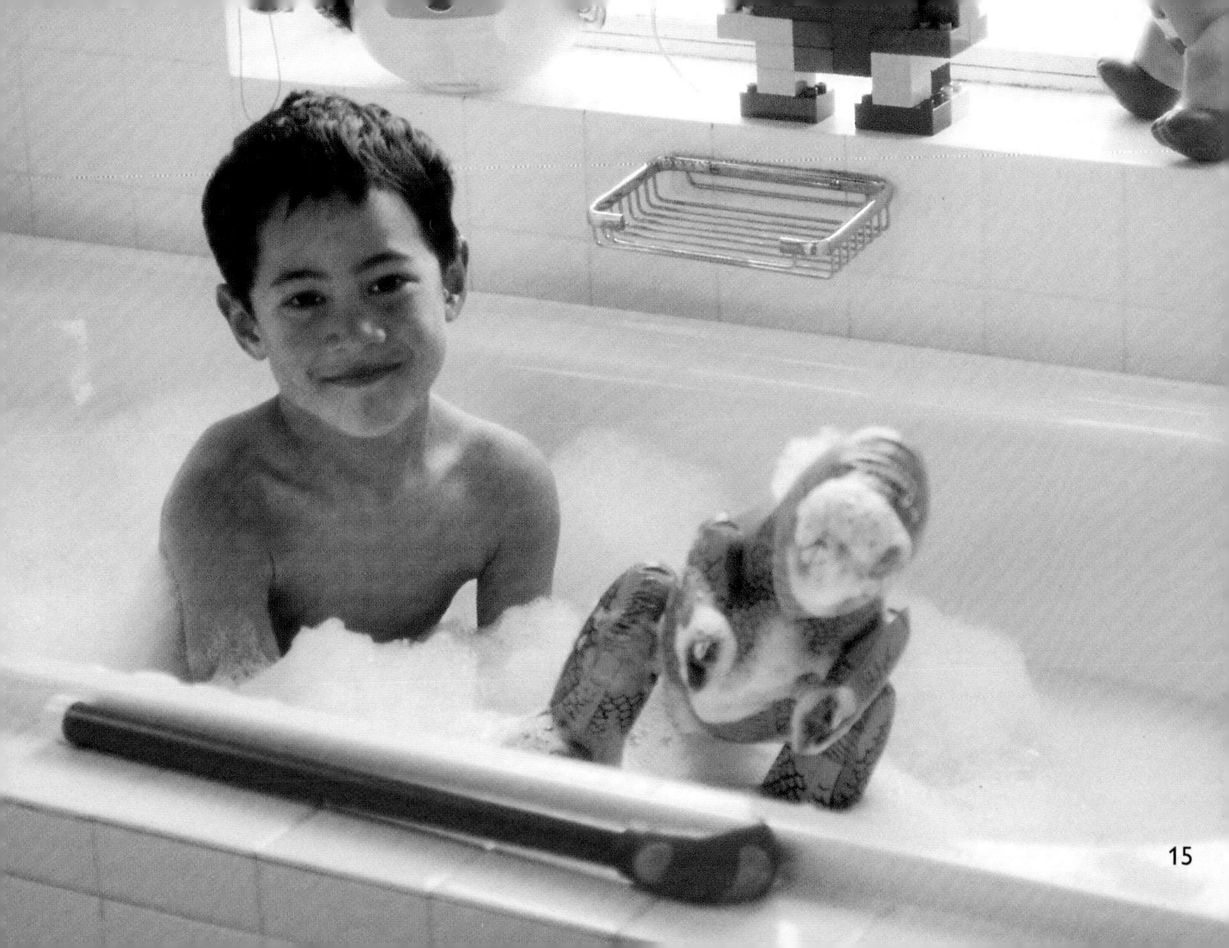

I am in bed.

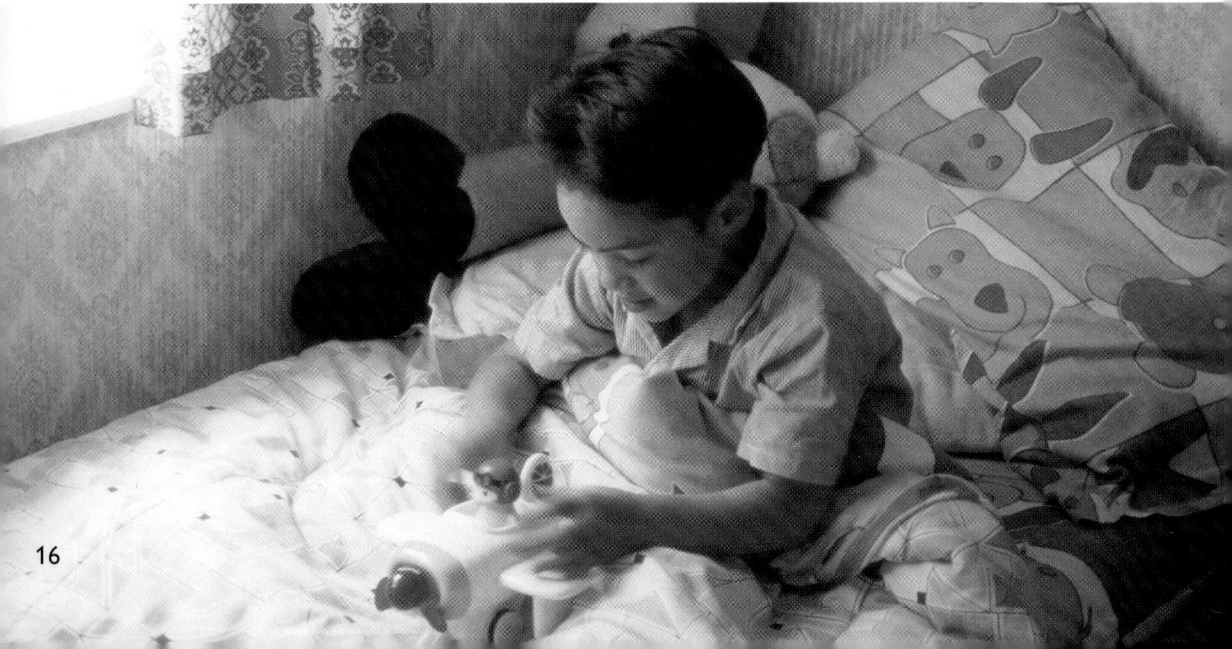